THE UNCONVENTIONAL GUIDE TO SURVIVING A PLANE CRASH

DON'T PANIC, AS IMPOSSIBLE AS IT SOUNDS,

IT WORKS.

Jerry M. Howe

Copyright © Jerry M. Howe

All rights reserved.

No part of this book may be reproduced or stored in any retrieval system or transmitted in any form or by any means, electronic, mechanical, photocopying, recording or otherwise without express written permission of the publisher

CONTENTS

- INTRODUCTION............................... 6
- OVERTHINK, PREPARE, EXPECT....................... 8
- DON'T PANIC................................. 11
- SEATS?..................... 14
- WHAT YOU WEAR............................... 16
- "THE PLUS THREE, MINUS EIGHT RULE"........................... 17
- SEATBELTS, USEIT........................... 18
- THE EVENT; BRACE YOURSELF............................... 19
- AFTER THE CRASH.......................... 22
- CONCLUSION................................... 24

INTRODUCTION

It's every airline passenger's worst fear. You are thrown back by unexpected turbulence. The drinks cart speeds by and collides with the back of the cabin. You're rapidly dropping altitude, and your seatbelt is caught between the seats. Oxygen masks fell from the sky, but you ignored the preflight instructions. As the plane drops at an unusual angle, people cry, plead, and clutch each other. You believe you are about to die. Chill !

There are actions you can take to enhance your chances of survival in the case of an air tragedy. Keeping a level mind in the face of chaos and terror is difficult, but crucial to your prospects. The clothing you wear, the luggage you pack, and where you store it are all important. Some studies even suggest that the seat you pick may be beneficial.

This book highlights all the STEPS and ACTIONS necessary to *literally* survive a plane crash.

OVERTHINK, **PREPARE**, EXPECT.

They might say you are being paranoid, but in the event of a crash, there are things you can do or could have done [hopefully not a "could have done" situation] to give you a better shot at making it out ALIVE. One of the most important things you can do to improve your chances of survival in the event of an aircraft accident is to know where the emergency exits are. Once seated, count the rows to the nearest exit in front of and behind you so you can find your way in the dark if required. If required, write the number on your hand in pen. By being mentally prepared, you'll naturally be more ready for physical action at a moment's notice. Learn the strategies below and incorporate them into your plan. When the time comes, act. Don't count on others to save your life.

Following are five *TIPS* that everyone should know before they get on their next flight:

- After you board, find the two closest exits and count the rows between them and your seat. In the event of darkness or smoke, feel the seats and count until you reach the exit row.
- Ready for the impact; The official FAA crash position is to extend your arms, cross your hands and place them on the seat in front of you, and then place your head against the back of your hands. Tuck your feet under your seat as far as you can. If you have no seat in front of you, bend your upper body over with your head down and wrap your arms behind your knees. Always stow your carry-on bag under the seat in front of you to block the area.
- Wear long pants, sleeves and closed-toed shoes. This will help protect you from glass, metal and the elements.

- If you're with your family, talk to your children about what to do in the event of an emergency. Divide the responsibility of helping your children between you and your spouse. It's easier for one parent to help a single child than for both to try to keep everyone together.
- **Pay attention to the preflight instructions, as all planes are different.** When the oxygen mask drops, put it on yourself first before attempting to help someone else. If you fall unconscious, you have no chance of helping your travel mate.

DON'T PANIC !

Many people who died in plane disasters may have been saved if they had not made certain catastrophic mistakes. Panic is the most dangerous opponent in a crash scenario. Keeping your wits and remaining focused will do more to rescue you than anything else. Panic is the reason why many people are unable to accomplish something as basic as unbuckling their seatbelts. The most frequent usage of a safety belt is in your automobile, with a push-button release. Remembering that the plane's belt has a pull-release isn't second nature in the heat of the moment. As a result, many crash victims are discovered still strapped into their seats.

Fatality rates increase markedly after the first 90 seconds following a plane crash. You can greatly increase your chances of surviving an airplane crash if you take a few moments to look around the cabin and think about what you might do to survive in the event the plane goes down. As researcher Helen Muir from Cranfield University suggests, you should be prepared to make the most of any opportunities near you for survival and escape.

Okay, here are a few **TIPS** you should remember if your plane is going down:

- In the event of plane fire, stay as low as you can and get out as quickly as possible. The smoke and fumes from a burning plane are highly toxic and more likely to kill you than the flames.

- The airline industry refers to the first 90 seconds of a plane crash as "golden time." If you're able to stay calm and move fast within this time frame, you have a good chance at getting out of the plane.

- If you make it out of the plane in one piece, get as far away as possible as quickly as you can and tuck behind something large in case of an explosion.

- Think before you drink. Consuming alcohol will slow your response time and cloud your decision-making.

- No matter what you believe can't be replaced, never attempt to take your carry-on luggage with you during an emergency exit.

- Don't inflate your life vest until you're outside the cabin. It will restrict your movement.

SEATS?

Where's the safest place to sit on an airplane? According to recent studies, the safest place to sit is in the rear third of the plane, with the last row deemed the safest because it's closest to the rear exit.

The 5 Row Rule: If your seat is within five rows of an exit, your chances of survival are substantially higher. The explanation for this is simple: following an aircraft crash, survivors travel an average of five rows to find an escape. Those who traveled more than five rows to an exit had a significantly higher fatality rate.

Which airline seats are the most dangerous? Seats in the center third of the cabin, as well as seats in the front third of the plane, particularly the first four rows, have a lower survival percentage than other seats (usually first class).

Are aisle seats more dangerous than window seats? A 2008 study by the University of Greenwich revealed that survival in aisle seats was greater than other seats, but highlighted that "being situated on the aisle gives just a modestly higher probability of surviving than not sitting on the aisle." According to a 2015 Time magazine investigation of aviation catastrophes since 1985, aisle seats are the least safe across the plane, with aisle seats in the center third of the cabin having the worst fatality rate. According to the Time survey, the middle seats in the plane's back third are the safest overall.

WHAT YOU WEAR

The clothing you wear on the airplane could help make the difference between life and death in the event of a crash. Wear a long-sleeved shirt [no buttons is best] and long pants. If possible, wear flame-resistant clothing [most western and work clothing retailers carry this, from Carhartt and other brands].

Polyester, nylon, and acrylic should be avoided because they melt at low temperatures and will stick to and burn your skin. Cotton is preferred because it burns less easily. Wool is better for flying over water because it does not lose its insulating properties as quickly when wet, but it is much heavier in the water. Don't wear shorts, dresses, skirts, or loose fitting, flowing clothing.

Wear strong, comfortable lace-up shoes with good soles and traction. Do not wear sandals, high heels, or slip-on shoes. Your escape from a burning plane could depend on it

"The Plus Three, Minus Eight Rule"

The rule's name alludes to the fact that eighty percent of all plane crashes occur during takeoff and landing - the first three and final eight minutes of the flight, respectively. During this time, stay aware and alert; do not read or otherwise distract yourself. Prepare to carry out your plan if necessary. Another piece of advice from the experts: wear your shoes during this time.

SEATBELTS, USE IT.

It's probably no surprise that passengers who wear seat belts during airline disasters have a substantially better chance of survival than those who don't. What may surprise you is how many passengers reported missing important time due to seat belt problems. Seat belts in aircraft, unlike car seat belts, usually do not release with the push of a button. While it's critical to wear your seat belt at all times during your flight, it's also critical to familiarize yourself with its operation, both visually and physically, so that in the event of an emergency, you can release the belt even if the cabin is dark.

Pull your seat belt as tight as you possibly can. Every centimeter of belt slack triples the g-force you'll feel in a crash. Pull the belt as far down over your pelvis as possible, with the upper ridge of your pelvic bone visible above the belt. This will keep you in place far more efficiently during a collision than if the belt was over your abdomen's delicate tissues and organs.

When seated, keep your seat belt on at all times, especially when sleeping. In most circumstances, you won't have enough time to fully awaken and respond before the accident, so make sure you're properly attached to your seat ahead of time.

THE EVENT; BRACE YOURSELF

In **MOST** cases, you'll be aware that the plane is about to crash long before it does. The cabin crew will almost certainly issue instructions; pay close attention and follow them. Use this time to review your plan, paying special attention to exit locations and distance from your seat.

If the plane crashes over water, put on your life vest but do not inflate it until you are safely out of the plane. Whether the jet is submerged in water or not, an inflated life vest will make exiting the plane more difficult. Swim out of the plane while holding your breath, then inflate the life vest.

Now secure any loose things in the area. Tie your shoes securely. Put on your jacket and zip it up. If possible, use a pillow, coat, blanket, or other soft object to cushion your head. Also try to pad your shins and ankles, if possible.

Both anecdotal and empirical evidence show that assuming the brace position or crash position as instructed in the pre-flight safety presentation prior to impact greatly increases your chances of not only surviving a plane crash, but reducing the chances of severe injury if you do survive. Fatalities in plane crashes are more likely to result from impact injuries than any other single cause. There are numerous reports of accidents where most passengers died and only a few walked away, reporting that they had been in the brace position at the time of impact.

The brace posture, when done correctly, prevents harm to the head, neck, and legs. It also helps to avoid whiplash, preventing you from flying around the cabin, and, to some extent, shields you from flying items. If you brace yourself before impact, you are less likely to be concussed and to sustain broken limbs. The brace position is possibly the most important thing you can do to survive a plane crash.

The brace position is performed as follows: To avoid shin injury, place your feet flat on the floor as far back under your knees as possible. Place one hand palm down on the back or top of the seat in front of you if you can reach it. Cross the second hand, palm down, over the first. Place your forehead against your hands. Do not bind your fingers. You can also rest your head against the seat in front of you. Lace your fingers behind your head, cradling the sides of your head with your arms. If you can't reach the seat in front of you or there isn't one, bend forward with your chest on your thighs, cross your wrists and grab your ankles. You can also grab your calves, with the wrists uncrossed, or lace your fingers behind your head, cradling the sides of your head with your arms.

Stay in the brace position until the plane comes to a complete stop. After the initial crash, there may be additional impacts to the plane.

USE THE OXYGEN MASK; BREATH AIR! :

If the cabin becomes depressurized, you have 15-20 seconds to put on your oxygen mask before you become unconscious. Put it on immediately, before assisting children or other passengers. You're no good to anyone if you're unconscious during an emergency.

Hold on to something, Anything! :

In the event of a free fall or if the plane breaks apart in mid-air, you should hold on to the most solid, substantial thing you can find. It may sound improbable but there are instances where people have actually ridden solid objects like seats, food carts or other parts of the plane and survived falls of thousands of feet without a parachute.

AFTER THE CRASH

Fatality rates increase significantly after the first 90 seconds following a plane crash. Follow the instructions of the cabin crew, but if they're dazed, disoriented, or dead, don't wait. Get out of the cabin as fast as you can and as far from the plane as possible.

If the nearest exit is behind you and accessible, ignore the human propensity to move forward rather than backward and move to the rearward exit. Assess the exit for safety—look out the window to see if there are any hazards present. If so, proceed to the exit on the opposite side of the plane or the next closest exit.

Leave your luggage; don't waste time looking for belongings that mean little in a life-or-death situation. If necessary, you can return to the plane later for anything that's salvageable.

The plane may explode or erupt in fire. Move at least 500 feet away from the plane in an upwind direction. However, stay in the vicinity of the crash site so that rescuers can find you.

Do you have any wounds that need to be cared for? If you're bleeding, apply pressure immediately. Assist others with basic first aid if you're able!

CONCLUSION

It's normal to feel a variety of emotions after such an experience, so eat well and get enough sleep to help you cope with stress.

And if this book helped or informed you in any way please remember to leave a review. Thank you and STAY SAFE! Cheers!